The Service Service Manual

by

Shel Shamus

Table of Contents

Introduction

The Current Condition

The Heart

Ethics

Why Be of Service?

What It Means To Be Of Service

What It Takes To Be Of Service

What Is Not Of Service: Selfish Love

Overcoming Ourselves

Personal Freedom

Personal Power

Morality & Service: Good & Right

Judgment

Equal Service

The Closed Circuit

The Current Condition – Part 2

The Big Bang

Fighting & Conflict

Enjoying Pain, Laughter, & Hurting Others

What Is Service

Two Axes

Romance & Sacred Union

Sex

Community

Giving & Helping

Strength In Action

Intuition

Creation

Unity vs. Separation

The Butterfly Effect

The Master Plan

0 - 1

Conclusion

Introduction

I should introduce this manual with the example of doctors and the Hippocratic oath. But instead, I will open it with waitresses. Most waitresses don't need to read this book. In fact, they should be teaching the course. Some doctors still need to read this. Waitresses know that service is a way of treating another that holds their interest alone in a given action or set of actions—as their job. It is a way to treat, serve, love, support, or help another. How many waitresses have you known to treat you badly, contradict you, not smile or act like they like you or enjoy helping you. Probably not many. They represent the perfect model of service—hence their newer title: server. You barely, if ever, notice their misery, trials, disdain for you, or anger. They *act* entirely selfless in service of you. Of course, they do it because at each and every table, in each and every moment, their livelihood, their tip, your choice in kindness, their life, depends on how you feel about them at the end of a half an hour or an hour. They survive on incentive at every single table; in every single interaction. It is profit based; survival and scarcity based. But they are a good model of true service.

However, as with most people in our society, they do it because they get paid better. It is an extreme example of incentive. It is an extrapolation of what every businessperson allegedly thinks and does over fiscal quarters, five year plans, and at the counter or register. They have to serve you, help you, to make a profit or make a living. Thus they treat you well, say thank you, and strive to provide for you at whatever level their business is.

We live in a selfish society. That's' why I have to use business as an example. Many, and it seems most, people would choose themselves and not really consider another's welfare, even at a small cost to themselves. We live in a world of extremely pure "selfishness." There is not a lot of heart in a lot of people. And there is not a lot of heart in the world that we have created at this point.

Of course, there's nothing wrong with taking care of yourself, loving yourself, and working hard for you and yours. But most people sacrifice others' welfare to excess— out of anything ranging from ignorance to convenience to enjoyment to use to cruelty. And this domesticated or savage norm reaches in to every avenue of our society— including service oriented professionals.

In for-profit interactions, service, guest, and client are common parlance for someone who probably would not otherwise give a crap about you, treat you so well, with much kindness, or concern for your well-being or feelings. Businesses are pretty much the only professionals who globally treat you well—or appear or purport to.

In non-profit ventures, however, where the client's interest is the sole purpose of the business, the clients are not so often treated so well. Government workers, welfare workers, social workers, police officers, legislators, the criminal justice system, the military, they do not have a direct incentive to treat you well or consider your interest highest even though they are directly charged with protecting it. Sure, legislators have to beat out one or two others with promises that usually end up getting broken or *compromised*, but mostly, they feel no incentive-based pressure, no *selfish* reason, to treat you well.

Government workers are notorious for being careless, uncaring, slow, and inefficient. Many hospitals, particularly in mental and behavioral health, do not treat you well either.

Government is the primary example and incidence of *non-profit* arms to hold you in this society. There are many, often private, non-profits who do hold their clients in high regard; even if in a paternalistic way. I do not mean to discount the many CEO's, board members, and social servants who do actually not let themselves interfere with their service and consider the welfare of their clients.

But most people in the world that we are constantly creating only care about you if it helps them. They will as quickly pull the rug out from under you for a laugh as they will sell you down the river for a buck. The going rate of love is pennies on the dollar at best—and your own joy at the expense of another at worst.

The Current Condition

Why do people act this way? Because they don't *have to* care*!*

Not only do you not have to care, the opposite is encouraged. All the way from the cool kids being the brutalizers to the big businesses exploiting entire continents for their own benefit. We learn it and live it early and often and ever. And this is what is rewarded. Is it what you learned in church or synagogue? No. But will is the ultimate splendor on our largely forsaken rock. But the worst part of it is that we do it to ourselves and each other. We choose domination, sabotage, and slander. The opposite would be using our hearts to see others.

The Heart

Our bodies are channels for energy, like radio receivers, with how we feel, think and act as our radio speakers: what channel we broadcast to the world around us. We are also part of a larger circuitry for energy and the reality, or dream, of the entire planet, and the universe. This energy flow, and its amount and quality, is mostly what make us feel how we feel: confident, insecure, excited, and such. Our bodies act as brains, along with our grey matter brains, with various energy centers vertically and elsewhere in our body that overpoweringly determine our conscious and unconscious reality: our dream.

At the center of this energy flow in every one of us is the central crux of our field, a regulator, or fine tuner, for our entire being; that which, more significantly than anything else, determines the quality and interaction of our being and how we interact with and treat each other: *our heart.* We can entirely modify our individual and collective experience of our world by allowing, or using, our hearts to regulate, magnify and connect our energies.

While this information about our energy and the quality of our connection with each other is not new information, it is surprisingly *not* well disseminated and might be largely underestimated, if even understood, by such a large portion of us that the reality, the dream of our planet, is largely affected in what should be an obvious fashion: we are all too often at war with each other, and ourselves, individually and collectively, in various moments, our lives, and as nations and creeds. Or, at minimum, we throw each other under the bus for any type of enjoyment, security, or gain.

Affecting ourselves through our heart, and the rest of our energy centers within our individual selves, we can actually affect the entire world's reality. We can contribute so significantly to living the reality of peace and love on earth, each of us *individually*, in our own lives firstly, and very directly, from doing so in our individual lives, collectively, that heaven on earth, as so many great teachers in the past and present have been directing us toward, is very possible *as a reality for our entire civilization*. What regulates this dream for us as people and as a culture is our hearts. If we practice seeing with love, the world starts to look a lot different. If we imagine ourselves in another's position, we understand. It changes the way we approach them. People like Ghandi, Marin Luther King Jr, Nelson Mandela, and Mother Theresa aren't known for revolutionizing industry, being wealthy, or being famous. They are well known for being lovers; saviors; saints. And people know who, in your community, is the local Saint. How many times at a funeral have you heard "I've never heard gossip or an ill word spoken by_____?" How do you want to be remembered? What kind of impact do you want to have? Who do you want to be when you grown up?

Ethics

Many educators and administrators try to inculcate a set of ethics into their respective fields of practice to ameliorate the attrition of self and selfishness in service oriented professions and institutions. Many do not. In social work school, they never stopped trying to get the "self" out of "service." I am not so certain that police officers receive the same level of education. And that ethics course that your congressperson took in law school twenty years ago seems a bit difficult for them to remember.

Everyone who is charged with serving another, from your senator to your social worker, should receive an education in what it means and what it takes to be of service. This is it.

Why be of service?

Why did you go into a service field? Are you a lawyer solely because want to make money or have status, or because you believe in the Constitutional ethic of defense. Do you act entirely and vigorously on behalf of your client or do you cut corners or take the easy way out.

Are you a teacher because you love kids and want for them a happy, functional life or was that the easiest degree and career option you could take?

As a social security agent, do want for the best of your indigent or ill clients? Or is it a good job that you can fart off at and can't really get fired from?

First, why be of service?

Because the kids, clients, community, citizens, and criminally charged are hopeless, in pain, needy, hungry, and lost without you. They are very real people, just like you, who are in need. They cannot function or live happy—or at all—without your help. If you were in their shoes, you would know why to be of service. If you were in their shoes, how hard would you want your advocate to work for you? It *is* that simple. But it takes a lot of awareness, work, and patience.

What it means to be of service?

Being of service takes as many forms as there are vocations, needs, and desires? True service can take place anywhere from the coffee shop, to congress, to coitus. The common denominator of service is being what the person being served needs. What it means to be of service is to be entirely for another, have the drive necessary to be of service, and have the know how to help—at least on the job.

The know-how is taught in college or grad school or seminary. It should be being taught from kindergarten on. But, alas, big business did not have that in their agenda for us collectively.

The drive is something that you either have or don't have. It could be commonly called a work ethic if you are in the service profession. And the desire determines whether or not you should even be in the field. If you do not currently possess these three, you probably shouldn't be in a service field—unless you want to open your eyes to being a true saint, even if in a smaller pond.

What it takes to be of service:

No Strings Attached or Mixed Motives

Our priorities, needs, fears, and resultant belief systems and action patterns dictate and explicate a variety of motives that vary within both self-serving and "other-affecting" to mix into a hodgepodge of conflicting and separate issues. And at a rampantly common level, many parents are quite selfish to the point that they sacrifice much of their children's development and wellbeing for the sake of their social life, their anger, or just their ignorance. True love, however, separates, sifts, rearranges in priority and meaning, and dictates a different type of drive and direction.

Without a clear "knowing" of where we, and others stand and how we relate, need, and love, our motives can be directly or indirectly conflicted and enmeshed between connective or serving and selfish or disconnected and/or destructive. That's why it can be advantageous, for those who do not feel the place of love all the time from which they act, to be aware of or examine our motives if we are to come from a place of divinity or love when interacting with or affecting others.

Mixed motives are those that are conflicting, often selfish vs. giving, that impede or pollute each other or one the other. We all have multiple motives in our lives: desires for ourselves and others; often-times mixed up and conflicting. If we are in a service field, we can shift our awareness and activity to make our selfish motives parallel or independent from our motives to help another so that they do not conflict (specifically relevant here as the selfish not polluting the service-oriented).

For example, it is not uncommon for people to offer a gift and then ask for something in return, if only a thank you. That is indicative of an over-investment in self and one's own attachments, or needs, or an expectation for a return on an investment in someone else. It happens at all levels.

Government agencies that are supposedly dedicated to protect and serve quite often have built in expectations of their recipients. Private, non-profit agencies often have an affiliation or sect that requires their clients to act according to their philosophy of life. Friends do this of each other. Spouses notoriously do this. Even parents who do not realize so, or the impact of doing so, so many times expect or require in a non-serving way for their children to give back to them in some way in exchange for what they are given—if nothing more than appreciation—though the parental model, if it were pure and unconditional, would be a good model.

Of course parents can require their children to work, or any other domestication that is serving of them, either out of necessity, or out of love, either way, gifting them with security and self-sustaining ability. But requiring any form of reciprocity not out of unconditional love and support, or absolute need, in any form of relational exchange, indicates an attachment on the part of the giver that basically means that the gift is not in fact "free" (and often not pure).

Service can entail an agreed upon exchange, as with a for-profit business, which implies that both parties are appreciative of something offered—something truly beneficial—by the other, hence the true exchange. This is one example of parallel motives—which is different from mixed motives that are intertwined and pollute each other. A business relationship generally involves multiple motives too, where a store or anyone in a contractual agreement has a known and expected exchange or trade. It is quite another thing to unconditionally love someone in any way.

For those whose business it is to serve others, like social workers, teachers, government agents, etc., their service truly needs to be in a place of love if it is to be beneficial for those being protected or served. A specific example would be a public servant, like a police officer, or set of laws, which have the job of protecting the public from harmful interaction, yet involve quotas or the desire for, and action-based, power and control or personal gain, both on the part of the civil servants and/or the public or special interests. These severely interfere with the purity—the benevolence—of the service that is supposed to be performed. The personalities and self-interest of those legislators and officers in power over us often interferes with the clear channel of protection and love that could be offered us and the rest of the world. And the private interests of the public or special interests who lobby or vote for the legislation can pollute the purity of the public domain also either in minority or majority opinion. A clean government legislates freedom and protects the private rights of and interference from its citizens and does not legislate opinion or morality as much as is possible. And the communitarian services that a government provides, safety nets, welfare, fire rescue, should be offered in total service and purity: love.

In many cases, sometimes dangerously, other times just selfishly or impertinently, an offering, or the energy of it, can be tainted or mixed with self-interest in a polluting or exploitative fashion, willfully or unconsciously, especially if it is accompanied by any coercion (like government) or is required by necessity.

The truth behind this is that nothing is truly not a choice if one is willing to accept the consequences of making another choice, or lack thereof. Police officers have a choice—or their captain has a choice—or the legislators have a choice—and the voters have a choice on how to require and how to protect and serve. But most people are not willing to be without or face the necessities thereof, thus allowing those who have, or those who enforce, to dictate their activity or well-being in a polluted and mixed fashion; often with self-interest interfering. Yet, in common society, with an implied social contract such as today's, where people want to live in a material reality that they can feel safe and secure in, preserving life and liberty, it makes sense to highly limit or highly regulate the impact, force, or influence of government or "public" servants and legislation—and to clean up the social services and agencies. This is unlikely to happen if we don't raise our voices collectively—our power—to require our public servants to be accountable to *us* instead of big business and personal interest. But if only a few take a stand, like some politicians and voters do, they will be scandalized or eliminated from power—with applied retribution to boot.

But being aware of how mixed motives, if not regulated by the heart, pollute our interactions and the services and protection we receive, helps us dictate our own actions and preserve ourselves from the enforced actions of others and provides a start for a more forgiving and more just community. An option is to increase the accountability of those in power, those responsible for our protection, and teachers and such. Another option is to pay the social servants and teachers much more to attract the finest from colleges that otherwise will be pursuing law careers. Another option is to utilize technology to initiate true democracy instead of representative government. Yet civil and general education (socialization) would likely need to be adjusted to reflect service, love, and common welfare (hence this book) instead of fear, polarization, demonization, and profitability—as we are nourished and manipulated with in the usually fear-based daily news: the daily, polluted baby formula that we are raised on.

Also, social and moral agendas add to the selfish agendas of politicians and other arbiters of justice, like judges and juries. We must be careful how we manifest our collective reality—our dream.

Receiving a gift or payment or even a thank you as a means of love or energy in return for the original service indicates a voluntary love-based reciprocity of sorts on the part of the receiving party, as is the case with donation-based or sliding scale service. And many businesspeople actually do care about you. Thus their mixed motives can actually be kept parallel.

Living and giving with heart can un-pollute the selfish aspect of giving, giving the giver the option to give with no strings attached. The parent-child relationship should be the prime example of this in its intent.

Of course, everyone has multiple motives, some of which mix into simple actions like love making, and making money. The key is for each individual or group to be clear within themselves and with each other about their goals and what they desire. Heart-based connectivity can insure that all parties are well served.

It so happens that a pure heart enjoys giving and treating others well. That is the ultimate motive. It is actually quite enjoyable and fulfilling to serve others. That energy gift in itself is very rewarding payment.

An open heart also facilitates understanding of a situation and performance of any function. It means treating others well, looking at others with attention to their strengths and potential, compassion for their suffering, and forgiveness.

What it takes to be of service

To be able to put aside yourself, your own interests, your own wants, your own wounds, to be a clear channel of love, of service, for your recipient.

What is not of service:

Selfish Love

Most people grow up fantasizing about a perfect, romantic marriage, often with one of them "saving" the other or both of them "completing" each other. In our world there is rampant "codependence:" emotional dysfunction whereby people offer "love" and "support" to each other, appear to be caring, to themselves and others, but really are acting out of fear, selfishly attempting to control or determine the outcome of another's actions to feel better themselves. They are not okay unless another acts a certain way.

The desire on the part of those who act in these "need-based," "caring" relations, is to feel safe or okay based on the service they are performing for the other. This classically happens in some of the most dysfunctional relationships and family systems, but it is a plague in our society and in almost all human relations as we know them. Our legal systems are based on debt and guilt; our marriages are cages for our partners; our families are often controlling and petty, if not abusive or neglectful. Our work and peer relations are often fraught with competitive character assassination (gossip). Our good friendships are generally the only relationships we have that have a chance of being string and judgment-free.

When a codependent person acts for another, he or she subconsciously or consciously strives for or expects a certain result or response. They have learned over time, that a successful skill in getting their needs met is to shower affection or service on another, to the point that they live by a "system" of cause and effect that they depend on emotionally, even if it is a fear-driven or unstable system.

Or, there is a habit of showering disdain or anger on the other out of a conscious or subconscious desire to control the other—really to appease a desire or fear of their own.

A hallmark of these types of relationships is one person "making" the other one feel guilty, through direct communication, or indirect body and emotional language. Of course, it is not actually an ability of one to actually "make" the other feel guilty (or anything else) as we are taught, but an unhealthy dance of codependence—the dance of action and expected result. It works because both believe in the dance, or "system," that they ascribe to.

Listen to most of our love songs and romantic movies and you will notice that we are literally plagued to our great and collective dis-ease in almost all of our relationships by this selfish love: codependence. And all news station feed us a complementary diet of fear, division and threat. Both serve to educated us all of our lives to be cauht in petty ad grand wars—to blame and control others at the level of the basic populace—keeping us scurrying about, running into each other like a pinball game; all to keep us occupied, uneasy, and striving for security and supportive of destructive and exploitative agendas. You can be sure that someone benefits from every news *story* we misinterpret; from every *terrorist* attack; and from every *crisis*. This can be avoided in our lives—with awareness; with reading between the libes; with seeing from our hearts instead of our guts individually, with concerted effort, and collectively as more of us join the ranks of those who instead ascribe to a freer love. However, the codependent, even if educated through fear or neglect, has great potential to be of the greatest service to the world—just by cleaning up her mind and actions.

The Present Moment

To be fully present and alive is the first goal of this path, accomplished by the mental and emotional labors that bear fruit later. There is great emphasis on the present as it is the only place that we truly are alive. But we must sacrifice much of our perceived ease of avoidance of our pain that creates the unnecessarily suffering-oriented aspects of our personality through direct confrontation and feeling, which seems like unnecessary suffering in the now, so that we can be freer and more pain-free later.

The emphasis on the now can only be fully understood by how trapped we are in our pasts, as indicated by either our current level of suffering in our daily interactions or our avoidance of things as we go about our business.

If we have problems in our relationships, for example, we are stumbling through the present, suffering overly, which is traceable directly back to or emotional wounds of the past and our resultant mental patterns of today—which combine to take us out of the present. Whatever issues we have take us out of the now; and take us out of love—and with authoritai. If we pay attention to how we swerve and curve around our issues and with our discomfort, we will notice how we are suddenly either thinking from a hurt place in our life or blanking out—either way, not in the now, enjoying life or being at peace. And as we continue to act out of the fears of our "baggage," we will gloss over peace and love: a handy service to those who use us for power and profit.

The goal of getting back to the present is attainable and worthy of having. It is difficult to explain how full life is without our wounds of the past. The peace and joy of that energy are astonishing. If you were to experience a moment of that with awareness, randomly, in the midst of an "average" life, you would know you had felt the true Nirvana. This is actually attainable—which you will come to realize as you do this work. That is the essence of the present moment. And to do that you must seize the day in this way.

Overcoming ourselves: Agreements & Cleansing

The crucial step, instructions for which are outlined further in this book, is to cleanse ourselves mentally and emotionally (our past traumas and fear-based reactions) so that we can feel peaceful and act completely volitionally, joyously, creatively, productively and connectively. It is only our internal "baggage" that prevents us from channeling and manifesting this life of our completely free choosing. True service is not possible weighed down by your own baggage or seeing through personalized or societal lenses that skew our view of the needy person in front of us that needs help or service (or would just be a good "free" companion).

The earmarks of our cleansing process are when we experience any emotional pain that we believe is rooted in our present interactions; the people, places, and things currently around us; arousing us; and angering us. We are actually reacting to our past domestication (like that of a dog), a false, familiar template that we place over our present. Our wounds, an image from our past, is generally observable as such by the disproportionate level of fear, pain, or drama we are feeling now, relative to the simple current events and interactions we are engaged in. This drama impedes our present or future. It is kind of like subconsciously like continuing to spend time in our past as we plod and suffer through the present. When this type of perversion of reality occurs for us, we are not truly free to choose, or even know the gifts of life in the present moments, as they pass right by us, for our energetic, mental, and emotional diversion, backwards and in truly unnecessary suffering.

Virtually everybody possesses these energetic "links" to the past, due to high intensity events that "taught" us a lesson (that we have carried too heavily and too far); and virtually everyone can clean their emotional and energetic bodies of these unnecessary and burdensome suffering-oriented energy and choice drains.

The process for doing so is intense (without judgment), or difficult (with too much meta-analysis of the thoughts and feelings) yet very possible to accomplish with persistent, directed effort. Involved is taking times to deliberately venture down the paths of our mind and emotion that we dislike the most for the sole purpose of allowing the pain to complete its path energetically: just "feeling" all the way through it without conclusion or judgment this time around—which happens to be what we did not do when we first made the agreements with ourselves that these suffering inducing energetic blocks are. We did not know any better at the time, and still may be avoiding feelings as such to the point that we are still creating these energetic blocks to this very day by not allowing ourselves to "feel" our emotional pain—as it has come to us through our experiences in life, starting when we were children (maybe being yelled at; maybe being ignored; maybe being physically hurt). A lot of anything that happens to people in life that we were not aware how to deal with partially or greatly traps us in our pasts, energetically, emotionally, volitionally (though seemingly involuntarily).

We "agreed" to these wounds—these energetic traps of our power—that are still draining and trapping us in our present lives. Much of the parts of our "selves" that do not serve us, whether we realize this or not, are actually "personality," or characteristics of us as individuals (though they are quite often repeating patterns among large numbers of us) that are merely energetic blocks of dysfunctional, suffering-inducing "agreements" (in that we had to volitionally trap that energy, even unawares, between us and ourselves which we used to keep ourselves safe). We have generally, at this point, way more than worn out their usefulness in our lives.

Opinions, over-thinking, judgment, and confusion arise from a mind clouded by all of these draining, painful, and conflicting energetic blocks and suffering-oriented agreements. We cannot form clean, clear, or adequately "true" perception, "thoughts," or beliefs accurately or productively without a thorough mind-body cleansing process.

One can "agree" to things that facilitate the process of self-renewal, like being careful and deliberate with our words, not taking things personally, not believing things that we do not have as verifiable, or "making assumptions," trying our hardest, and committing to be okay with our best efforts, in these and all endeavors and, thus, not judging ourselves. And then we can eventually transcend even these agreements when we reach the point where the reality is that we have arrived at the place where these agreements come from and fully internalized their lessons and transformed ourselves, and our lives, at which point externalization becomes the reality.

Through the guidelines in this book, you can reduce the amount that your involuntary agreements affect your well-being, freedom and personal power, liberating yourself to a life of great energy flow, peace and joy. And at the point that we are finally clear, we will not be hindered by false or unnecessarily painful perception, reaction or belief—and it is only at this point that we can fully and proactively construct our reality to the fullest.

Personal Freedom

Personal freedom is what we need to be happy in ourselves and to become pure servants. We cannot be weighed down by our own demons. Freedom is a word that used to be thrown around a lot. Sometimes for good reason; other times to pull the wool over our eyes. Now, it, and liberty, remain in some of the patriotic songs and advertisement lingo that we never hear properly. It is a worthy political ideal and an even more worthy personal one. It interplays with personal power in that one must embody one to appreciate and enjoy the other. This is very different from the freedom that comes from having a material cornucopia at your behest. And it is very much having an energetic one. And it is very different from the freedom to control the people, places, and things around you. Essentially, it is being able to make a clear, voluntary choice at any given juncture, in any situation, without being overrun or over-guided by fear: fear of retribution; fear of loss; fear of the unknown; and without the over-attachment to any type of mental, emotional, or physical high. It is being a clear channel for love, no matter what pinball game you have been in, no matter what situation you are facing, no matter who or where you are. It is not needing to negotiate for any reason—or need in any way—because you are okay, or not, anyway: okay enough to not make a harmful, or unloving, decision in any way. No matter the consequences. And okay enough to always (or pretty close to always) make a loving one. That means even in the face of death, and all things short of it. This is very different than the easier softer way—yet the path is so overwhelmingly clear, when we are clear, that one may never understand how they made another type of decision. And the reward is, somehow, in the decision and action itself. It's not called pro-action for nothing. This freedom is realizable. It is in your grasp, though you may not know it yet—or you may not know that until you make a decision and take an action or a stand in this type of freedom and power: the type of power it takes to know yourself and your path—even in the face of a lifetime of oppression, abuse, neglect, judgment, punishment, or internment.

We are all Mandelas, Kings, Ghandis, Theresas, Buddhas. Many of us just have not felt the love flowing through us to realize that we can be just as great; as effective, as true on our personal path. Working through to the point of channeling love that vectors dedication and understanding and action. It requires self-love, empowerment, and leads to true freedom, which allows loving service.

This freedom is acquired through awareness that what we are thinking, what we believe, and what we feel are generally lies.

Personal Power

Another avenue for being cleanly of service is personal power. It can overcome our demons so that we have the wherewithall to be of service even with our baggage or lenses. We have a chance to act *as if* we truly were in a clean and clear place of love for another and her needs.

People often consider power the ability to control other people, places, and things. People think that if they have all the stuff they need in their lives, or all the people they need in their lives, or the right mate or the right job, making the right amount of money, that they will feel great and be "happy." This is not to say that those things cannot be rewarding, or lend themselves to a fruitful and joyous life. But being truly happy is a very different endeavor than arranging people, places and things outside of yourself to the point that you feel okay inside. And it generally doesn't work well like that at all. The best case scenario in a life where someone successfully does this is one where they are adequately distracted or addicted to those outside entities and forces to not feel the baggage and suffering that they, if they are anything like a "normal" person, have been carrying through their entire lives and, regrettably, missing the point that happiness has always been, and continues to be, an inside job.

It is the energy that we are leaking and is trapped in our mind-bodies, through the suffering agreements and cords that we have had, and continue to make, that prevent us from truly feeling peace and joy, and don't allow us to find our fulfillment or adequately manifest our true purpose cleanly.

Personal power, among other things, is when we have all or most of our power back *from ourselves* in the way of both willfully and through inaction not falling into the traps of our inner experience (still likely perceived as our outer experience). Our energy flow will be much cleaner, more fluid, and more powerful, making us able to actually accomplish our lives in a way that we could not previously do, or, oftentimes, even dream was possible. It is then that we feel true power—which is true comfort: the ability to be okay no matter what the outside looks like—which puts us in a position to make the choices that we will then know are the worthy ones.

Morality and Service: "Good and Right"

The heart processing our energy allows us to perceive our world with understanding and compassion. It is the actions that stem from this understanding that have been limited and categorized, independent of a given situation, and called "good" or "right." It is not an accident that "good" and "right" involve so many caring and positive actions. But a lot of other, more "random" stuff has been added into the lexicon of goodness and righteousness. And using the ideas as a rigid and unchanging code of conduct, or book of law that finds people "guilty," or "bad" or "wrong," is a very limiting, confusing, and punitive way of approaching the possibilities for connection, clarity, and resolution. Good and right would naturally spring from an open heart—a caring and clean perspective—that sometimes differs or changes from time to time, depending on the circumstance—and does not follow a rigid code of conduct.

It is also not a coincidence that the "seven deadly sins," seven assessments that are extrapolations from perversions at the energetic level, are considered not "good." They are representative of fear-based selfishness that result in unnecessarily "sinful," or disconnecting, behavior. Lust, for example, without connectivity is often considered less fulfilling than "making love."

And jealousy, for example, is a fearful perspective (or experience) whereby a person's lack of self assuredness is projected on one or more other persons as blame toward them for spending time with another—when really the reality is that one person's involvement with another has nothing to do with another person at all, even if two of the three or more are more intimately involved. Jealousy, or self-consciousness, unlike what it could describe, is not an accurate reflection of any other party, though it does indicate a wound, or wounds, experienced by the individual who is feeling it. It is a projection of one person's insecurity about him or herself, blamed on another.

Heartfelt energetic attitude and aware action naturally results in actual "good" or "right" behavior, no matter how those actions appear—not living according to a set code of behavior, because the situations, actions, and individuals can change and still be loving or "good," though they may not always be perceived as such.

A way to define "good" or "right" behavior or intent, instead of according to a code of conduct or book of law, is "love" or "loving."

The "loving" action in the moment is always the "right" action in that moment. It does not change. And it having been the right move does not change—nor does the fact that we did or did not do our best. Sometimes there are various or even conflicting loving or "right" moves—and sometimes it may seem that one loving action may outweigh another. There is great subjectivity and room for interpretation (and misinterpretation by others). There are utilitarian perspectives as there are times when the inherent "rightness" or love of an action is outweighed by a longer-term or broader benefit. The question of a loving action being more important than any unloving action that should yield other loving benefits is a crucial question. Maybe doing a loving thing in spite of energy toward the opposite will always pay off in the face of utilitarian activity. Maybe there are tough calls that need further review.

Maybe there is no perfect truth. Tough calls, split decisions, and acceptance of all of the heartlessness in our world may need to accompany the pro-action and perserverence of the move toward love.

Sometimes we might decide to stay a right action based on other possible right actions at the time or in the future, if we can be certain about that future reality. That can change the way we look at the current right action—or we can have the perspective that there's no time like the present and let our future selves take care of our future situations. The universe presents us with opportunities for right action all the time. So, yes, the opportunity will arise again—and again—if we do not take it now. Sometimes the lesson will be more taxing the more times it has been presented to us unanswered. Other times, our inaction will appear to us in the future to have been no more hurtful than it is to ourselves for not having made it—or facing the consequences of not having made it. Of course, it is possible to ignore any form of assessing our place in the universe and our current or lifetime relationship to it—what our impact may have been on helping another—but that will then be our opportunity and lesson.

Judgment

A huge obstacle to being of service and truly loving another is judgment. We have learned a lot of ways to shame or guilt ourselves and judge others likewise. Judgment will often preclude our ability to help another, as our emotions, activity and motive will be mired in a mud of polluted motives or lack of motivation to help (as our recipient just isn't "good enough" or "worthy" or chooses the "wrong" things in life). Of course there is the extreme example of helping a murderer being counterproductive to our common interest. But most judgment polluting service falls far short of this and insidiously sabotages our own ability to help.

For example, a social worker that is charged with helping an indigent client; but the client smells badly. So the social worker avoids her and does not provide the same level of service to her—either as she turns off the social worker personally, or is less valuable to or able to fit in with society. If the resources are there, and nothing significant is lost by helping her, the job should be done equally well—even and especially if the client had ill will toward the service provider. When we become vengeful or personal in our jobs—and in our lives—we, and they, lose. "Self" has no place in service.

Equal Service

Men and women need not be treated differently. Black and white need not be treated differently. Rich and poor need not be treated differently. We have our judgments about different people being different and differently deserving. These are the beliefs that ether can be abandoned or at least ignored. As a social worker, I had a client who was berating me as a cracker, etc. as I was endeavoring to help him find treatment and sentence mitigation. I chose to not let either my personality or the client's personality affect my level of service to him. The principle that supercedes the personalities involved is service: love. We need never have a preference that overrides our charge or ability to serve.

The Closed Circuit

A tragic and hopefully temporary situation in our humanity right now is the closed circuit. We are so often minimized in our connectivity to smaller and smaller circles, oftentimes revolving around just a couple friends, our families or, worse, just ourselves. How many of us have yearned for connection to others or great or creative endeavors and have eventually relegated to a "simple life" for its ease or its availability.

The tighter we spin, with distractions, with dead-end or wholly self-interested careers, with only our closest companion(s) or children, the further forward in time and energy we push our potential, impactful connectivity with our entire universe and collective healing—maybe toward retirement (we'll just get a boat and play on the lake)—or maybe all the way until "next life."

But how many others like we were, or are, are yearning for us to figure out how to connect with them, to help them or love them, just as we wanted to be helped at one point—before we settled for "what we got."

And not only are there those waiting for us, there is another us inside of us that has wanted for so long to be let out of her or his shell, in so many simple ways every day, that that person may have relegated her or himself, too, to "what's for dinner?" or "where are we going on vacation this year?" or "I hope he/she gives me that for Christmas."

There is resolution for when you think you're ready to take it up a notch: herein lies a process for just that, instead of spinning in our smaller and smaller circles.

When you know how hard life can be; how disconnected you can feel; how bad the fear and pain are, or you have just never left the homestead much—then you know how bad others can feel, or how under-served. You can just look at them and see so clearly their pain; their nervousness; their confusion—or you wake up so numb that you don't even know what you—or they—are missing. It is then that you realize how important it is to love others instead of treating them badly or disconnecting—how much more important it is to treat them well, be there for them, and offer help and service, rather than think of ourselves and our needs or live in fear-based limitation. It is in this new place that we know how much we can love each other. And it is always a choice, even if we must come back to it.

Creation myths from all sections of the world speak of an initial separation. Some refer to it in terms of masculine and feminine; others the void and the material; others order and chaos; or symmetry and dance; or stillness and movement; or acceptance and courage. Many would consider our "condition" on planet earth, and maybe the entire universe, a disconnected, disenfranchised, and, at best, discontented disarray.

This reality, juxtaposed with our romanticization of romance and love can be interpreted in between as a real drive to connect. Helping others, love-making, and creating to share should let us know what we might be here for: to love; to serve. Service is not something about inferior and superior. It is about true worship: *being* purity of love.

Our true desires to love and be loved are real—and the resultant beauty and feeling good of hugging, cuddling, sex, friendships, family, and community are a real interpretation of our mission on this planet. But we cannot accurately know how, when, and why to do this without a process of "finding ourselves," involving undoing all of the damage and blocks of the channels of energy and vehicles of life that are our bodies and energy fields and habits, or patterns of action. That is the purpose of the lessons in this book—and the real goal once we do. Get out of our closed circuits.

We can open ourselves to a much larger circuit. You might be amazed how much larger our collective circuit can be.

Maybe this book will help you find the place where you will be able to feel others—and yourself—if, at first, through seeing through their eyes. Clearing ourselves will clear the channel and allow connection.

The Current Condition – Part 2

We have been limiting ourselves in our energy and activity, via our habits, our energetic disconnection with life, and with each other through energetic blocks, limitations, and ties: all voluntarily though unwittingly. It is voluntary because we implicitly learn to act or react in a certain pattern, based on our training as children and adults in reaction to our caregivers and each other. Really, there is no other way it can be when we unconsciously agree to our conditional relation to others and our world. No one can force our energy or activity, internal or external, closed without our implicit or voluntary agreement. We have "learned" throughout our lives how to avoid "pain," or the discomfort of heavy emotion such as fear, sadness, and anger (and all of their variations and combinations), through avoidance externally which disconnects internal fluidity, feeling and love, at the time and permanently, locking in hard lessons as a circuit pattern inside our mental, emotional, and energetic body.

In other words, we have relatively or very difficult or traumatic experiences growing up, as young adults, and as adults that we have learned from, ignored the magnitude of the lessons from, or not simply felt all the way through in their moments, in favor of distracting or numbing out for comfort's sake at the time. But those feelings of fear, sadness, and anger that we ran from the first times are still trapped inside us waiting to be expunged through feeling them, reconciliation, and acting in spite of or in accordance with.

When we were slapped on the wrist, or worse, any times in our lives, or went through extreme heartache or defense, and we could not or would not let ourselves fully experience that pain, we established an agreement each time with ourselves that "that" was how we would react: incompletely—which adds that energy that was left for by us for ourselves previously for later interactions and transactions that are similar or related to the ones where we established the erroneous circuitry. By the time we are adults—or even young adults—we have so much "baggage" that we carry into every job, relationship, and relationship with ourselves that we can barely be human.

That's where a need for love comes from: what we could call our original, pure, state, before we pollute and weigh down ourselves and our energy and contribution to our own lives and the lives of others with the baggage that we have unknowingly picked up and held all the way to now, almost all of which is excess. These are our current agreements: from how to act, to how to look, to how to have sex, to how to interact, or work, etc. We don't even know what they are, or that we even have them weighing us down, other than the fact that we are not supremely happy and functional all the time. Any "issue" in our lives that last longer than a moment emotionally or in any other way, not resolved easily, indicates this reality—and could not even exist if we are willing to go through a process of the recovery of our divinity, or spirit, we could say—leaving us free, peaceful, joyous, and passionate in a way that cannot even be imagined until we have done the work to recover, and arrive in such a dream that blows away our current state and comprehension.

Thus is the origin of the term "agreement," from our relative domestication on this planet—our interactions with our caregivers, our peers and teachers, our employers and employees, our partners and spouses, our entire society, who suffers from the same type of condition and reinforces it in itself and us daily. We have been socialized—like dogs—to have all of our beliefs, which guide our actions and emotional state. Yet we are so far down the wrong rabbit hole that we will fully adhere to and promote this book of law, justice, punishment, and, most of all, limitations and cruelty and exploitation—all coming from our socialization and, often, from our "gut" instead of our "hearts." The gut indicated fear. It os the location of our adrena glands and our digestive, consumptive systems: our fear and avaricial locuses. Our hearts, our bosom, can be more the source of our consciousness—and, thus, our world.

That is where we agree to re-agree on a new perspective, with new behavior mentally, emotionally, spiritually, energetically, and, then, connectively with each other. It is a utopian dream that is already real for some of us that you are being invited to join. Thus, love through perspective change and, then, action.

The Big Bang

If not to consume and use the planet for pleasure and pain avoidance, why are we here? And why are things the way they are? And what do we do about it? These are good questions to ask if things aren't supremely satisfying and supportive in your life. If they are sad and sundry. If love is lost and pain is king. If apathy or dissatisfaction are yours. If restlessness and irritability or anger define your life.

Science and mythology both tell of how our universe started as one, God, the divine, and then exploded, or separated at birth, into all its little pieces. Is it any wonder so many of us live according to a romantic myth of our own? Waiting to be completed? Waiting for a hello? Wanting a hug, or for the emptiness inside us to be filled? Waiting for sacred union.

We are all Romeo and Juliet, waiting to be re-united. That is why we see so many movies and hear so much music screaming out what we have been deeply troubled by: our separation from each other and our true selves and all, and in, creation.

Is it any wonder that our reality is so dualistic in nature: male, female; masculine, feminine; left, right; right, wrong? We are a dualistic dream trying to right itself into oneness again: union, re-connectedness. That is why we love. That is why we have been given these bodies, this equipment, and this mentality. What do you think God had in mind for us? Is it not obvious?

If we are unhappy, helping ourselves is not a bad idea. But if we need help from others, how often is it there? And how consistent and good is the help? Or are we only consumption, only selfish, instead of everywhere—or osatisfied wherever we are. How about every time we set ourselves apart from others; every time we think "us" or "them?" How do we feel then? Safe? At risk? Angry? Afraid?

There are those for whom conflict is a necessary component of our universe—their world for us. "Divide and conquer" is not a familiar phrase for no reason. Many feed off of our fear, anger, and resultant judgmental and punitive paradigm. They benefit from us monetarily, in power, and in satisfaction. Some of them you know. Some of them you don't. Some of them are you.

We pervert God's dream for us and our own true nature when we buy into the consumerism and conflict reality. That's not to say that all consumption or conflict are without cause; but probably only about 10% of it is worthwhile or crucial (and you might be surprised which 10%). When we buy the bombing, the bear, and the bull, we stop dreaming and we settle for having lost our true love. And we don't even know why every day we are dissatisfied, distracted, or dull.

Because we need to love. Yes we must start with ourselves. But there should not be that great a cost to helping oneself. And it need not harm or take from another. Pure capitalism, without manipulation from the monied elite, is a good system where to help yourself you have to help another (the media notwithstanding). Communism wasn't a bad idea either. Both have been corrupted by those in power to all of our loss. Even anarchy could be palpable if we thought with love instead of fear, scarcity, and power: more! But after we help ourselves, then what? In an ideal world whre service just happens organically on all levels, alongside self-love, there needn't even be this discussion. Maybe this world exists in a parallel universe, maybe only in some's minds. Maybe in our own future.

Our lost love and service heart-mind battling our violent, consumptive, scarcity-based, and aggrandizing reality is the battle between entropy and gravity. It is the original break; the original dualism trying to realign. We are fighting with ourselves and each other, in spite of ourselves and each other, to reconnect: with God, with each other, with ourselves.

Fighting & Conflict

Thus far, invariably, conflict arises in life. Many times, the cause is worth fighting for, despite our ire; and many times the war is pointless. Once we clear ourselves and have a grasp of our mind and energy, fighting will almost cease to exist, as, with our hearts turned on, or in the habit of love and service, we will logically and naturally care for ourselves and each other to the point that most conflict or conflicting "needs" will cease to exist. We may still have battles within and outside of ourselves, and until then, it is important to be able to defend or proactively prevent any type of scourge that can be avoided with fighting.

Fighting is a valuable skill though not always a necessity. Until these lessons are internalized and manifest by the world, conflict will arise. Being able to resolve conflict, defend ourselves, and pre-imptively strike out of necessity are all wise talents to possess, both physically and verbally. But fighting is a digression from true strength in resilience and non-reactivity.

Physical fighting and weaponry are talents and deterrents that are becoming less pertinent as we shy away from obsession with material things and scarcity and move more into the world of the enough.

Sometimes we find ourselves avoiding situations and people that may very well be advantageous to confront or relate to, in favor of our safety—not that every potential confrontation must be created or faced. And it's nice to not be or feel bullied by or in fear of another or one's own position. You don't have to learn to fight to not be afraid of confrontations and consequences, but learning to fight may be a result of standing firm and not being bullied.

Verbal and written acuity can provide resolution or defense, and energetically flatten conflict or solve problems that are either physical or mental in nature.

Our material reality can be a harsh place.

Collective defense and protection, or community support in a fight, will be our best asset as we transition from the world as we know it and have known it to the connective and mutually supportive world that we can create. We do often find also, that the heart pillow diffuses many a conflict, both internally and externally.

Enjoying Pain, Laughter, & Hurting Others

On a microcosmic level—in a lesser way—we are doing the same thing at home, at work, and in our little communities. If others' disdain, anger, sadness, strife or dissatisfaction gives you joy, this chapter is for you. And if you find slapstick comedy humorous this chapter is also for you.

Sometimes we can learn to enjoy pain: ours and others'. This is often a welcome relief—and if it is our only option, not to be judged. We might see a painful situation of someone else's and laugh, or laugh at ourselves. In this way, we are alchemizing a tough reality, if at a low level.

And we might "know" from association, that certain things are "preferable" to the pain of our wounds—like ball-shots, rough sex, or ridiculing others or ourselves. This is not to say that one should judge these as "bad" either—just that there is an choice in every one of these escape hatches of our pain to either enjoy a harsh universe—or, perhaps, to change it. Sometimes we may not be able to escape our old loops, thus alchemizing them in this way is best. But we are able to act, think, and promote a more loving way. It may not be as enjoyable yet, but it will be if you keep fighting for it—to the tune of freer and more fulfilling and more loving life experience for you and those you affect.

And it is key to see what laughter does. It lets escape energy before it touches that which hurts—or that which we see in another that brings up pain for us that we would rather focus on another by laughing at them—as is the case with anything we do that is directed toward hurting another. At an un-aware level, enjoying trauma, forming trauma bonds, and promoting pain is normal—and careless and divergent—both to yourself and to others—as it maintains a wound (though in enjoyment).

If it is done as a scaffolding to a freer and more loving place, good luck to it. If it never lets escape the wounds of you or others—inflicting crucial or permanent damage—increasing scarring or maintaining a wound—it is imprisoning (perhaps not as much for you, but perhaps greatly for others).

Thus, gouging and laughter can be a product of maintaining and re-inflicting wounds too. Even things that were not a problem to overcome before. And some would say that a tendency to choose other than a pattern of attack is weak where the habit of overcoming it—again and again—is stronger. Preparation for reality is love. Perpetrating it isn't. If your philosophy serves you and humanity, more power to you. If not, thanks for contributing to our enslavement and sickness.

The wounds aren't the real person, though being okay with them is. Laughter isn't the real person either. Choose your enjoyment carefully. Your corner of the universe will reflect or be created accordingly. Being weak is all in the interpretation: one can see toughness externally or internally. And one can see love as weak and attack as strong—or the reverse.

That is basically what we are doing when we hurt another— is letting out energy on someone or something else before it hits what hurts in us. A habit of hurting, or neglecting others can be a result of a lifetime of wounding. And intense anger can cloud our assessment of what is best to do in a situation, even though it may be a function of our energy bodies dictating how to react to threat.

Even self-defense can be an outlet that prevents fear from taking over too much, though that would be what the fear would be motivating us to do. And self-defense is not "wrong" either—nor is "turning the other cheek." These are all decisions that can be better made when one has become as close to a "clear" channel as possible.

Often, many of our issues are buried pretty deeply, even under laughter. Laughter is often a side-valve for energy in our mind-body consciousness that is actually being avoided or repressed. So make sure to think hard about everything that makes you laugh, cry, angry, and, most of all, afraid. If that does not dissipate all of your wounds, you might benefit greatly from putting yourself into relatively safe situations that bring up the emotions you have been running from so that you can feel your way through them. Just remember that in those situations, at that time at least, it is generally way more important to feel through them consciously in your mind-body, than to "resolve" the situation itself. That is why you put yourself into it in the first place! So you can face life without your emotional blocks!

If you have a great deal of power in life, if you feel "on top of the world" and depend on that daily charge from exercising or playing with that power, you are not as loving or service-oriented as you would be if you exercised instead your spiritual self in the way described in this book. Of course you don't "have" to do anything you don't want. But you don't yet realize that you actually *want* for yourself a more fulfilling path—where your current path has presently led you: here—instead of just getting high off of power. It might be hard to imagine anything being more rewarding than playing chess with the world—but that reward does exist. I would explain it to you now but you wouldn't understand or believe it until you felt it yourself—which I am offering you. But to each her or his own.

What is service?

It is love. What is love? The word love usually means romantic love to people—or familial love. There is a greek term, *agape*, that describes a divine love which could describe the intent behind this manual. Love can also be interpreted as the basis for and the reality of real world actions ("acts of love") that can range from romantic, familial, acts of worship, to giving to the poor or helping your fellow human or animal.

Love is also energy and is a reinterpretation of and involvement of other energies in the way that any desire or wish or hope or drive can be interpreted with heart energy. If our heart is turned on, everything we do or react to enters and comes out of us in a different fashion. That is why it is so important to reinterpret and regulate our activity and our "channel," with our heart.

Love is a natural occurrence for us as humans, but is not always the case for all of us. Damage as a child and from each other adds up. But our hardwiring is one of love. We are quite fortunate to have this as our reality. It is something that we are born emitting and need reflected from our caretakers in many ways to allow our progression as humans from child to adult.

As adults, we can direct our loving intent for ourselves and our world, and to children, if we choose to have them, or take care of them, to help them actualize as loving and productive and creative humans when they reach this level of being. Our ability to love is a product of our collective energy, as individuals and, eventually, as a planet. It is very much related to how other energy flows through us, which is limited by our personal and collective traumas, which are a collection of limiting and conflicting beliefs connected to matching energetic blocks in our activity that perverts and prevents our energetic flow. This manifests as how comfortable we are within and as ourselves, often a reflection or pattern of the conscious and unconscious interaction of our and others' energies, how loving we are with ourselves, and how comfortable or pro-active we are with loving others.

We can determine how cleanly our love or energy, in general, flows through and within us toward others with deliberate choice resulting from deliberate awareness. Our feelings and actions will follow either unconscious or conscious living. Which do you want?

Two Axes

There are at least two axes, with two sides of the coin for each, in action and interaction on this planet. That is to say, there are at least two coinciding and, at times, conflicting forces at play in our universe. There is the self-sufficient, or selfish, and the loving/connective, or conflicting/disconnecting.

These two axes can describe our human, physical reality and our spiritual, or divine, reality. An energetic way to look at it could be our lower and upper halves. Our lower half determines our physical: our security, sexuality, and sustenance. Our upper half determines, or embodies, our connection, creativity, and interaction. Our heart bridges the two, crossing these two axes; this dual reality: the physical and metaphysical—or material and spiritual.

These two axes are related in our reality and in our perception and manifestation of that reality like matter and energy flowing back and forth between each other. They can be coldly felt and related, in a selfish and exploitative manner, or the blend can be regulated and alchemized in our center by the heart. The heart, if utilized, transforms this physical into self-love and the connective into service, or love of and for others.

The heart-mind regulates and reinterprets the entire system, making disconnected activity and connection more impeccable. It helps redirect our selfish motivations and behaviors through our hearts to create a different way of viewing our self interest—and living life. We can allow our motives for career, sex, consumption, romantic, and other relationships, communication and interaction, thinking, learning, and connectivity to our universe to easily be fulfilling and giving—loving.

We can have a loving relationship with ourselves and each other in our work life, in our sex lives, our self care, our marriages and families and peer relationships, the way we speak to each other and think and educate ourselves and each other, our creativity and, most of all, the way we treat each other.

Interaction with the universe without the translation of heart-mind can result in fearful, aggressive, exploitative, addictive, aggressive and, in general, overly conflictive, or even murderous, interests for us as individuals and groups.

Our motives are cleansed by the heart. "Deadly sins" become loving actions. This transformation within each of us, or the lack thereof, reflects a larger macrocosm in our world and, possibly, the entire universe.

If, for example, there were two warring factions in our universe, those who appreciated and fostered connection, learning, communication, loving relationships, peace and joy, creativity and empowerment, opposing those who sought control, knowledge, disconnectedness, over-indulgence, rape, and power, likely motivated by disconnected self-based fear and scarcity mindedness and isolation, there would be an opportunity to contribute to which way we wanted to influence and interact with others and live ourselves—and affect this universe.

The self-interested, fear-minded and overly moralistic/legalistic would likely use utilize hierarchy, standards of right and wrong, fear, anger and rage to define their universe which manifests as conflict, war, degradation, disrespect, addiction and self judgment: all forms of addiction in the mind, body and activity, desperately and eternally trying to take in from the outside what they believe they are missing from within.

The fact that we live in a world that is teetering between heaven and hell, equally so in everyone, moment to moment, begs the question: which way are we going to put our effort; our personal contribution. The change begins within—and extrapolates and gathers with other parallel motion and energy—to motivate a larger scale change that we each can contribute to. The two axes can, in essence, become a cross—or a crux—in our becoming a world of love instead of war.

Romance & Sacred Union

As our lives and sex lives begin to flourish, we will often be called again to relationship—the consistent attraction to others romantically—that will have taken on a new meaning through this process.

Most of us have experienced relationships and the obsession therein. We have gone from crushes to first loves, through heartbreak, to being repeat offenders and exes. Throughout these lives we have experienced tremendous desire and what we have called heartache or heartbreak. For many of us, we have felt that our or others hearts or sex drive are overactive or insufficient. We have pitted ourselves against our partners and done a great deal of blaming and finger pointing. At times, we have realized our own blocks or inadequacies and taken them out on our mate—or we have blamed ourselves primarily for the collapse of something that we over or undervalued.

There is another way, which we will see clearly when we are of sufficient clarity, strength, will, humour, good will and love. It will come when we are no longer selfish yet we are able to direct our own lives sufficiently—when we are giving yet not needy for a response—and when we find someone that we feel comfortable cooperating with in partnership toward the end of our own and his or her personal freedom and empowerment.

Romance is fuller (than casual or just sex-based relationship) developed partnership that generally involves connection, cooperation and/or support at all eight energetic levels. Sacred union is when we find partnership that embodies a full acceptance, non-judgment, and trust that can open the doorway to the most intimate of support-based, mutual self-actualization. It is meeting each other on every level of energetic exchange for the mutual benefit of all involved. It is at this opening that true, full partnership occurs.

People in this type of relationship will encourage each others' benefit and personal growth with extreme wisdom, heart, confidence, and security, not threatened by the other(s). In this type of relationship, we are okay with and by ourselves, even though the idea is to improve upon our tightest circuit and desire to share our lives with and by inclusion of another or others.

Sacred Union can be with a mate, partner, or anyone in your life, if you desire and have the courage and ability to be unconditionally supportive, giving, and honest without harming yourself or them. And when people come together, especially in a sacred fashion, great things can come of it.

Sex

Not easily understood, but certainly known and felt, is the drive for connection sexually. Connection is beautiful. There have been and are many things that get in the way. You could say our socialization and habits as humans and children and having bad upbringing play too big of a part. Women are told they are sluts. Men are told they are oppressors. Hygiene plays a part. Forgiveness plays a part. Passion, allowed to flow without our minds getting in the way—even using them pro-actively—and, of course, energy flow, play parts.

We can increase energy flow sexually to increase the field and ease of play, more or less, to change the game, by liberating our minds and then liberating our bodies equally.

This will lead to blowing our minds before we blow it with our bodies.

Pretty much everything that gets in our way of enjoying ourselves and each other sexually can be solved by letting go of our judgment and victim mentality.

There is dominating sex, lovingly connective sex, and service-bearing sex. We can even switch roles or, for some, sexual orientation in any given moment—at least in practice. And we can enjoy it with just about anyone with our minds in order and our love reigning first. Our physical, diet and exercise habits can improve our sex lives. Our commitment to ourselves and each other, at least in the moment, in these ways—and maybe others—will likely, most of all, do the trick.

And our sexuality and biology mirror our needs and desires. To fill a hole inside of ourselves or be hugged sweetly are not coincidental realities and metaphors for our needs for ourselves from ourselves and each other, at times.

Sexual connection is one of the greatest phenomena of love. And it is a perfect metaphor for the benefit of giving. Indulging in love, serves both parties. It is what we are built to do with and for each other and ourselves (am I giving away the secret to the universe too early?). New life comes from it, both inside ourselves, with each other, and in the form of all of our children.

And we can add energy to each other or help drain anxiety and angst from our lives through sexual intercourse, not to mention commit ourselves to endearing connection, adding a foundation to an otherwise loving affair.

Community

Community is created by individuals. Community follows their actions and beliefs. Society is one example of that. Our planet is another. Our friends are another. Our marriages and families are another. You decide what type of community you want to live in by the way you choose to act. If you choose to be of service—to be love—your community will be that. This will be the case both as your paradigm and reflected in those who you attract to be around you. There are exceptions to this rule, but they are all the more reason to be of love and service. Changing the planet into one of love is much more fostering for ourselves and others. Strength is valuable in battle alone. Practicing that strength should be done with care.

Giving & Helping

It is enjoyable and beneficial to give and help under most circumstances, even in a limited lifestyle or environment. But serving divinely occurs when we have removed our energetic blocks, personal interest (or importance), and can cleanly channel our and the universe's energy to the end of the greatest good of ourselves and those around us.

We actually cannot know what is best for someone else, or generally even ourselves very well if we are still energetically blocked, living in the past, so to speak, with the baggage in suffering agreements from our lives.

When we clear ourselves, we will have the ability, confidence, and know-how to truly be of service to our fellow human—and, likely, we will have the courage to do so—and enjoy it.

We could just all fight it out and see who wins. But that just leads of a battlefield full of blood and the need for a do-over.

Strength In Action

Giving and helping cannot truly occur, nor can any of this process, without strength, or acting in power. While it is true that we will have less power until we complete this process, we will be able to muster a great deal of human strength, as we are survivors at worst, picking ourselves up by our bootstraps it may seem like at times, just by a strong enough desire for change and true peace and joy, as we are potentially much more than survivors in reality. We will back this desire with everything we can do to make this happen, finding it in ourselves to achieve this goal with a knowledge that this transformation truly is what we can be gifted with as our human inheritance, ripe for the taking of any individual who wants to claim it, and has the wherewithal to force themselves into this cleansing fire and stand the flame.

Intuition

Many of us are familiar with the feeling of intuition or a "gut feeling." Others feel that they are being led by a divine force. It may be that they are both true.

It is also possible to trust oneself as a vessel or channel of divine knowing that can detect the deficits and outpours at the various levels of human interaction and in their world in general.

Detecting that something is "wrong" may be an accurate reflection of another's plight at the moment, or a manifestation of one's own blocks. After adequate clearing, one can "go out on a limb" and complement another's struggle, in fear, anger, sadness, "stuckness," with appropriate love and energy.

Likewise, we will be able to understand the draw from others for love and connection, and for ourselves, and be able to meet ourselves and each other there.

There are different channels of these verbal and non-verbal connections and inter-flow can occur. They involve security, sexuality, danger, will and action, love and compassion, communication and consumption, and universal connectedness. These are channels for understanding, or intuiting each others' and our own needs and possibilities.

We have the choice between unconsciously reacting to or complementing and growing into and with each others' energy. With the insertion of conscious purposeful connection and complement, regulated by heart, we can consciously determine the course of our individual and collective dream.

Knowing how and when to act, when to change your course, when to interrupt someone else's dream, or when to be "big" and draw a crowd or go so against the grain that no one would understand until possibly much later is about trusting yourself and your relation to the universe. This comes from the aforementioned cleansing of your energy body and mind and will be a result of your assuredness in your place and choices; always in the moment, even with careful planning or extended action.

Oftentimes you will have help knowing and other times you will have to know and do without the same reassurance from outside yourself. Sometimes doing your "piece" is easy and sometimes very much not—both being just as valuable to your universe. Sometimes it's easier when it's harder when its only you—and sometimes it's easier to delegate. When it involves standing up in a crowd, it can be most difficult, even when you now it's "right." And, as more of us stand up in those crowds, with and for each other, the balance will shift so that the crowd will be those doing what is hard, right, against the grain, and those that are not will be the minority.

If you think you are the only one standing up in the crowd—but you know it's right—just know that there are others, in your past, your future, or right beside you, in spirit or elsewhere, doing the same thing with you—and that it will work out for the common good, as difficult as your path might seem in those moments.

When we are clear, are able to see and do this. Our point in the web in each moment becomes more and more obvious and available to us the cleaner we become. That is when we know what is best for ourselves and/or those around us with more certainty in accordance with, in time with, and in conjunction with the all-knowing-being-doing that connects every being and moment in every instant at all times: that which has always been, and continues to offer us opportunity after opportunity to be at our best—and to make a difference. There are always at least two directions. Regulating our point on the web with heart will lead us in the direction that will result in ultimate connection, creation, and our best interest.

Creation

What comes forth from a clear channel is also sacred. Creation and connection go hand in hand and result in everything from children to art to architecture to power plants back to farming and play.

We all have some type of experience creating from our lives. Many of us have painted or written. Many of us have formed businesses and others are carpenters. Some of us caretake the eldery. Others caretake nature. Many of us are parents and others are teachers. All of us plant our loving creativity on this earth.

As we clear ourselves, we find that creation is more pure and deliberate—more easily seen and done. There is much that we no longer need to seed or grow, but there is much that we could not do either of before that we now will be able to accomplish.

Sacred union bears fruit in this way, as does individual planting and dancing. We will know from our hearts and connectivity at the point of clarity how and what to intuit and thereby create in our connective life.

Unity vs. Separation

Amidst all the parallel dichotomies expressed in our universe, reaching the point of cleanly being able to truly act toward and be in unity is of primary importance and ultimate cruciality. We currently live in a world of artificial, biological, cultural and belief oriented divisions that, if we continue to contribute to, we will be choosing our own dissection, collectively and energetically.

Men and women are not truly at war. Blacks and whites and other races are not truly at war. Catholics and Protestants, Christians, Jews, and Muslims, and Communists and Capitalists are not truly at war. It is individuals and oligarchies that are disconnected from their own real peace and joy who fight for control of each other, and pit us against each other, through ourselves, based on whatever we believe differentiates us, based on whatever makes us insecure—at least in our minds and body-minds.

We have now, and will have even better, the opportunity to support and help each other, first by chelping ourselves and each other—seeing the similarities between us instead of the apparent differences; basing our perspectives of ourselves and each other on something besides a material reality or belief system; knowing what we feel—that "they" feel it too; utilizing our own human experience and reality to connect with each other instead of letting our disconnecting energies, like anger and adrenaline and being drugged, lead us to separate ourselves from ourselves, which is what we are doing every time we tell or send off someone who is not threatening us, either directly or by omission of consideration, communication, or love.

We can see our own pain as a reason to support others, and, thereby ourselves in the end, or as a reason to lash out and make our personal universe smaller and smaller and more and more stabbing and confining, both inward and outward.

We can see others' weaknesses and vulnerabilities as something similar to ourselves, something to protect or assist, as we would love them to do, or as something to exploit. It does seem to all come back to us in one way or another—and that would be the point of choosing unity. Safety is not all it's cracked up to be—at least nothing like mutually assured protection and love.

The Butterfly Effect

Every action we take has an effect. Every effect has another effect. Service, altruism, and love spread. The seeds you sow, though many fall fallow, grow in others who then re-sow these seeds. Yes, we are fighting a current of use and exploitation, but even their hearts can be affected eventually. Even without giving with expectation or control, we can know that we are putting more ripples into the streams, ponds, and oceans that we live in.

The Master Plan

When a person decides to become a Vegan to be kinder to animals (not cage them; not kill them) and find sustenance and drive toward the altruistic, his health strongly follows. There is a huge statistical significance to this truth. Heart health, body health, and mind health follow Veganism. Though I just use Veganism as an example, it is the metaphor that altruism, kindness, compassion, service, and love to others parallels love for self. When a person decides to be kind and loving towards his fellows, his planet, and his universe, the universe reciprocates. That doesn't mean that everything in his life will look and feel like he expects perfect to be—but it is in fact what perfect will be. The things that happen in his life; the serendipity; the fortunate twists will always be in his favor. Sometimes there will be hard pills to swallow, but there will be a spiritual reality that will favor him, as it favors a saint along the proportion of your love toward your universe. So, imagining yourself in another's shoes is more than a mental exercise—a story or belief to help you make more loving decisions and actions. Knowing that you are that man or woman in need, just in a different body, makes you that sacred cow. Good feelings will develop and follow, giving you an immediate reward. Universal respect will generally follow, giving you a more loving social network and brotherhood. Your romantic relationships will change into much more fulfilling ventures as you get reflected back the type of person that you become—or change to people who are more loving like you are or will become. Good fortune will likely be yours (I've seen and heard about it a million times—from some of the worst criminals who've turned their lives around simply by giving up their criminal ways and becoming of maximum service—ending up with lives that far exceed even what they would have selfishly wished for early upon their spiritual shift). And universal love will likely follow. By that I mean spiritual things that you may or may not be on board with or be able to yet believe—but things like good afterlives and fortune in reincarnation and heaven can actually become real for you. All of the world's religions have some understanding or faith in this, though many a lay person may not. For the uber-rational, just know that you have hedged your bets and reaped the rewards of love and being of service this life. And when you flip that switch on to love for love's sake—with no expectation or need for return—you will never again need to understand any of these reasons. Your life will become the most rewarding possible from the inside. Helping others actually helps ourselves. Just like sex.

0-1

Our sexual reality, our technological reality, the forces or axes in our life, and, possibly, our universe, reflect a simple dualistic—or, actually, simplistic "one choice" reality: yes or nothing. This choice is interpreted in every culture as an order from chaos (and back) or a freedom to symmetry (and back)—as opposed to the perverted interpretation and reality of control and consumption and addiction.

It can also be thought of as an original point of creation exploded into the disorder, entropy, that we currently find, yet the pieces pulling towards each other, gravitationally, to reconnect—and create again.

When reaction goes by the wayside, there are really only two choices: non-action or pro-action, peace and joy, stillness and connection—despite all appearances. Discomfort and suffering can be a thing of the past with good student-teacher interaction and effort, be the teacher individual, collective, or the universe itself.

Hopefully all things relevant will be clear and we will perpetually be faced with the repeating choice: to rest or to act. I am confident that, at least in our universe, this choice will be laden with love if we so choose, a fortunate product of our having hearts to regulate the convergence of all of our axes and intersections.

Conclusion

When the waitress learns to love serving—and the lawyer loves defending, the government worker loves representing or providing, and the policeman loves protecting and serving—we have almost arrived. When everyone else feels that they are safe, lovable, loved, independent (or supported) and we all agree on love over fear, we have arrived.

It is in this that the journey is the destination; that the means are the ends; that you and I are safe and free. It is now that peace and joy become our lot—instead of just that corner office, that corner lot, or that corner plot.

www.ingramcontent.com/pod-product-compliance
Lightning Source LLC
Chambersburg PA
CBHW051711170526
45167CB00002B/630